Sleepy Little Owl

Howard Goldsmith

Illustrations by Denny Bond

LEARNING TRIANGLE PRESS
An imprint of McGraw-Hill

New York San Francisco Washington, D.C. Auckland Bogotá Caracas
Lisbon London Madrid Mexico City Milan Montreal New Delhi
San Juan Singapore Sydney Tokyo Toronto

©1997 by **The McGraw-Hill Companies, Inc.**
Published by Learning Triangle Press, an imprint of McGraw-Hill.

Printed in the United States of America. All rights reserved.
The publisher takes no responsibility for the use of any materials or methods described in this book, nor for the products thereof.

hbk   1 2 3 4 5 6 7 8 9 KP/KP 9 0 2 1 0 9 8 7

ISBN 0-07-024543-6

Library of Congress Cataloging-in-Publication Data applied for

Acquisitions editor: Judith Terrill-Breuer
Manuscript editor: Ellen James
Designer: Jaclyn J. Boone

LAND4

For Gingin Chen, with affection
—H.G.

LITTLE OWL was a tiny screech owl. His feathers were soft and fluffy, with flecks of brown and yellow. He lived with his mother and father in the tallest tree in Owl Wood, in a nest made of twigs and grass.

During the day, the owl family slept. At night Mother and Father Owl went hunting for food. Little Owl stayed home, snug in his nest, waiting for the time when he could go out on his own to play.

One morning, just before bedtime, Little Owl decided he wanted to play with the daytime animals. Mother Owl told him, "Night owls play at night and sleep during the day. Now it's time to hop into your nest and close your eyes."

But Little Owl had other ideas. He tucked his head under his wing. With one eye open, he listened and waited. When Mother and Father Owl were sound asleep, he hopped over to the nearest branch. Then he took another hop, and another, and soon he was down on the ground.

The green grass made a soft carpet for Little Owl. He jumped and
hopped about, looking for friends who were wide awake and ready to play.

Just then Little Owl saw a small meadow mouse darting through the grass.

Little Mouse was frightened when she saw Little Owl. She knew that owls hunted
by night, but she had never met one during the day.

"It's my bedtime!" cried Little Mouse, running into the woods. "You won't catch me!"

"I'm not trying to catch you!" Little Owl screeched at her—but Little Mouse had disappeared.

Before he knew it, Little Owl was getting sleepy. He had never been awake in the daytime, and the bright sunlight hurt his eyes.

Then Little Owl heard a strange noise: RAT-A-TAT-TAT, RAT-A-TAT-TAT. Looking up, he saw a woodpecker drilling a hole in a tree.

Little Owl said to the woodpecker, "I am so sleepy. May I rest in your nest?"

The woodpecker stopped his tapping. "I have no nest," he said. "But you can rest in this hole."

Little Owl hopped up and tucked himself inside the hole. But the woodpecker's bed was made of wood chips drilled from the tree. It wasn't padded with soft grass and leaves like Little Owl's nest.

"This is much too rough for my feathers," said Little Owl. He thanked the woodpecker and hopped on his way.

Soon Little Owl came to the edge of a pond. A frog sat sunning himself on a lily pad.

Little Owl said to the frog, "I am so sleepy. May I rest in your nest?"

The frog answered him with a croak. "I have no nest, but you can rest on a lily pad, like me."

Little Owl hopped onto a lily pad. He tucked his head under his wing, all set to sleep.

The lily pad felt damp under his feathers. The water rippled and rocked him back and forth.

"This makes me dizzy," said Little Owl. He thanked the frog and hopped on his way.

Soon Little Owl met a chipmunk. He yawned and said, "I am so sleepy. May I rest in your nest?"

"I have no nest," said the chipmunk. "But you may sleep in my burrow underground."

Little Owl squeezed himself into the chipmunk's hole. He closed his eyes and tried to sleep. All around him there were piles of acorns, nuts, and seeds for the chipmunk to eat.

"It's much too crowded in here," said Little Owl. He thanked the chipmunk and hopped on his way.

Little Owl was lost. Nothing looked familiar to him. The daytime animals were friendly, but he couldn't stay awake to play with them. He longed to be in his cozy nest of grass and leaves next to Mother and Father Owl.

"If only I could find my way home!" he cried.

Little Owl hopped along until he bumped into a tree stump. He was so tired he could go no farther. He found a soft bed of moss to rest on and fell sound asleep. Little Owl slept the whole afternoon and dreamed of home.

15

When evening came, Mother Owl and Father Owl woke up. They stretched and yawned and looked all around them for Little Owl. But Little Owl was missing!

Mother and Father Owl flew off at once to search the woods.

16

Down below, a mole was climbing out of his hole in the ground. When he heard the owls flying overhead, he was afraid Father Owl was out to catch him.

"Don't run away!" Mother Owl screeched loudly from above. "Please, have you seen our Little Owl?"

"No," answered the mole. "I just woke up."

"Thank you," said the owls, and off they flew.

Next they saw an opossum hanging by her tail from the branch of a tree. She was just about to bite into a crunchy crabapple. Mother Owl and Father Owl called to her, "Please, have you seen our Little Owl?"

"No," said the opossum. "I've been asleep. And all I can see from here is crabapples!"

"She's no help," Father Owl whispered to Mother Owl.

The owls flew on until they spotted another night animal, a raccoon. The raccoon was poking around outside his home in the hollow of a tree, looking for some nuts and berries to eat.

"Please," cried Mother Owl. "Have you seen our Little Owl?"

"No," said the raccoon. "How could I? I've been sound asleep all day."

Now Mother Owl was really worried. "Wait!" she said to Father Owl. "The night animals can't help us. Little Owl left home in the daytime while they were fast asleep!"

"So let's ask the day animals," said Father Owl. Then he opened his eyes very wide. "But now it's evening, and they're all sleeping!"

Mother Owl and Father Owl flew through the dark woods, screeching, "Wake up! Wake up! Has anyone seen our Little Owl?"

"I saw him," said a sleepy woodpecker. "He headed for the pond."

Mother Owl and Father Owl flew to the pond. There they saw the frog sleeping on his lily pad.

"Wake up!" Mother Owl cried. "Have you seen our Little Owl?"

The frog hopped up in surprise, landing in the water with a splash.

"I saw him," said the frog. "He headed for the willows."

Mother Owl and Father Owl sped over to the willows, calling, "Wake up! Wake up! Has anyone seen our Little Owl?"

The chipmunk peeked out of his hole in the ground. "I saw him," he said with a yawn. "He headed for the meadow."

Mother Owl and Father Owl flew off, looking down with their sharp nighttime eyes. Finally they spotted a tiny shape nestled in a bed of moss next to a tree stump. It was Little Owl! He was fast asleep.

Mother Owl and Father Owl swooped down and hugged Little Owl.

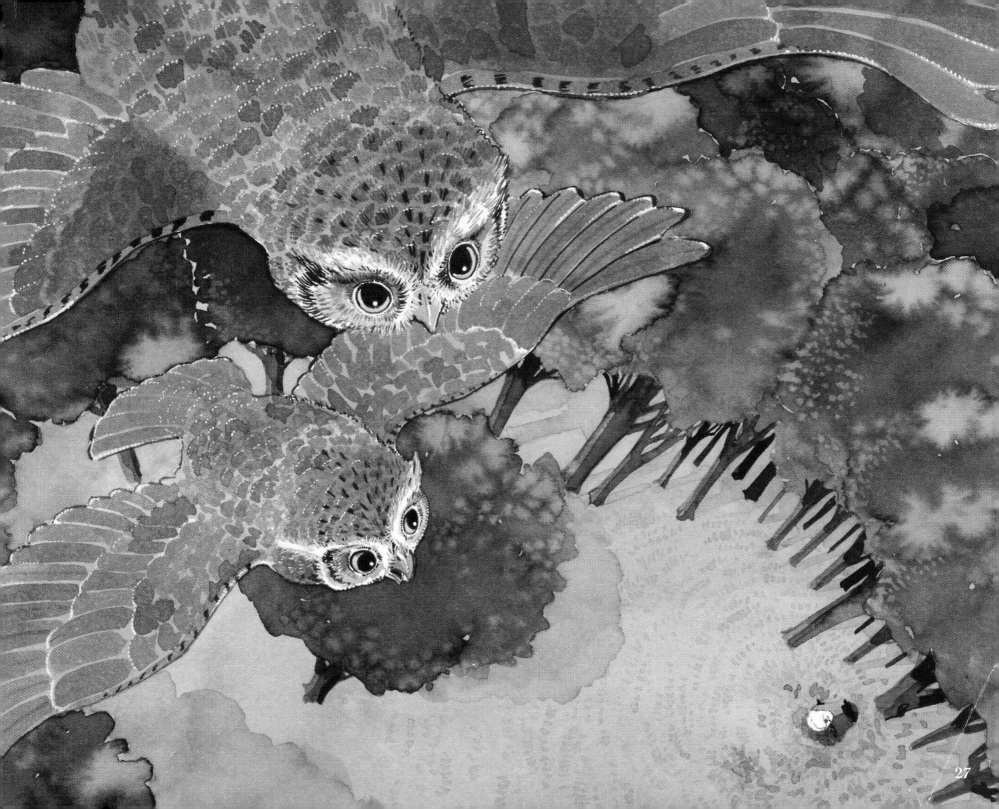

Little Owl hopped onto Father Owl's back, and all three of them flew home to their nest of grass and leaves high up in the tallest tree in the forest.

"What an adventure!" Mother Owl said to Little Owl. "Did you make new daytime friends?"

"I tried," said Little Owl, "but I couldn't keep my eyes open."

Pretty soon, night settled in over Owl Wood. Moonlight spread over the treetops. Stars came aglow in the sky.

All the day animals were sound asleep. But not Little Owl. He was wide awake, and now he knew that nighttime was his time to play!

Think About It!

Did you know that every time you read a story again, you can learn something new? Let's try it.

Scientists call **nighttime** animals, like Little Owl, "nocturnal." **Daytime** animals, like the chipmunk, are called "diurnal." You can remember these words because nocturnal begins with **n**, like "night," and diurnal begins with **d**, like "day." Can you tell which animals pictured in the story are diurnal and which are nocturnal? (Check your answers with the list below.)

Animals in stories sometimes speak, but everyone knows that real animals don't "talk" to each other the way we do. Can you think of other ways that animals communicate? What are some of the sounds they make? How does your dog or cat tell you things?

"Camouflage" is a special protection some animals and insects have. Their colors blend in with what's around them, so they can't be seen. Why do you think they want to be invisible? Can you find an insect hidden by its camouflage on the very last page of this story?

See how many of these animals and insects you can find as you look back through the story of Little Owl's adventures. (Then check your answers below.)

ants	Japanese beetle
beetle grub	katydid
bullfrog	ladybird beetle
butterfly	painted turtle
cardinals	pileated woodpecker
cicada	rabbit
click beetle	red fox
cloudywing moth	spotted newt
dragonfly	sunfish
earthworm	tadpoles
elk	water strider
field mouse	whitetail fawn
grasshopper	winter wren

Answers:

Nocturnal Animals
mole
opossum
owl
raccoon
red fox

Diurnal Animals
chipmunk
deer
elk
frog
newt
rabbit
turtle
woodpecker

Answers:

ants 8
beetle grub 13
bullfrog 24
butterfly 4, 7, 30
cardinals 6
cicada 4
click beetle 7, 30
cloudywing moth 28
dragonfly 11
earthworm 12
elk 23
field mouse 7, 13
grasshopper 7
Japanese beetle 19
katydid 19
ladybird beetle 9, 30
painted turtle 20
pileated woodpecker 23
rabbit 15
red fox 22
spotted newt 11
sunfish 24
tadpoles 24, 25
water strider 10, 11
whitetail fawn 14
winter wren 15

30